Raised By Mountains

EMBER BIRCHALL

To my summers in the mountains…

CONTENTS

DAD'S CASSETTE TAPE

For the first eighteen years of my life, these twenty-two songs played on a loop each time I went to my beloved caravan in North Wales. It would feel wrong if I didn't share these songs with you as you explore the mountains with me.

Dance The Night Away | The Mavericks | 4:24
Where Do You Go To (My Lovely) | Peter Sarstedt | 4:44
Je T'aime Moi Non-Plus | Serge Gainsbourg | 4:22
Fire | Arthur Brown | 2:54
Long Live Love | Sandi Shaw | 2:42
Michelle | The Beatles | 2:42
Green, Green Grass of Home | Tom Jones | 3:05
I'll Never Find Another You | The Seekers | 2:42
Don't Throw Your Love Away | The Searchers | 2:16
Mr. Tambourine Man | The Byrds | 2:29
San Francisco | Scott Mackenzie | 2:59
You've Lost That Lovin' Feelin' | The Righteous Brothers | 3:45
Reach Out I'll Be There | The Four Tops | 2:58
You Don't Have to Say You Love Me | Dusty Springfield | 2:48
Bad To Me | Billy J Kramer & The Dakotas | 2:21
A World Without Love | Peter & Gordon | 2:40
Do It Again | The Beach Boys | 2:22
Sunny Afternoon | The Kinks | 3:35
All Or Nothing | The Small Faces | 3:05

Blackberry Way | The Move | 3:41
With A Girl Like You | The Troggs | 2:08
Mony Mony | Tommy James & The Shondells | 2:46

1 WHEN I WAS YOUNGER

When I was younger, my stomach would fill with butterflies whose wings would beat in time with my ever-increasing heart rate as I grew more and more excited at the thought of going to the caravan. I'd be riding shot gun in my car seat with my teddy bear Birchy, slapping my knee and bobbing my head to Mony Mony by Tommy James and the Shondells as it blasted through my dad's cassette player, and I'd watch as he did the same. You see, back then, dad saying that 'we're going to the caravan' meant that this was going to be 'our time'.

Our time where there was no signal for phones and we would laugh and smile. We'd go swimming, go to the beach, go to the Wednesday Market over in Pwllheli, all accompanied by the same twenty-two songs on his cassette. But now, now the butterflies have been replaced with knots as the three-hour drive fills me with a kind of anxiety that I wasn't ready to grow up for – and the cassette is gone.

Growing up, the caravan used to be this perfect place, full of adventure and open skies, fields perfect for summer nights spent playing manhunt with my friends. Now it has become a haunted house filled with flashbacks of her chemo-stained pillows, his secret cigarettes that I pretended not to notice, and learning to cry myself to sleep without making a sound.

Since she passed away, nine years in September, the garden in front of the caravan that she loved has also died, the caravan is filled with the dust that she became, and the ties between us have frayed. You grew angrier, and I grew inward. Now I no longer have the confidence to race through the mountain tops the way I used to run to the swings. Like the woodpecker, my voice hasn't been heard for years as I no longer sing along to the songs on dad's cassette tape.

1Birchall, Ember. 23 Apr. 2020.

2 DRIVING TO THE CARAVAN

These days, when the cinema in Widnes and Fiddlers Ferry Power Station fade from view, my phone is plugged into the car playing the same twenty-two songs that made up my childhood car rides to the caravan. For as long as I can remember, dad had a cassette player in his car, but he'd lost all but one of his cassettes. He always blamed my nana, saying she threw everything away without thinking, but knowing him he probably stored them in a special place where he won't lose them, then forgot where that special place was.

A few years ago, when he started looking into getting a new car, I transferred all of the songs over onto a CD, bringing the likes of The Small Faces and The Move into the twenty-first century, but then when he got the car he has now, I put them all onto a USB stick. It's strange how that one collection of songs has seen the evolution of technology purely because I wouldn't know what to do if we were driving through Caernarfon and my dad wasn't quizzing me on what the French lyrics in Michelle (by The Beatles) meant.

It's strange the traditions that build up over the years. When he talked about selling that old car, I knew I had to keep those songs alive somehow for our long drives to the caravan and back.

2Birchall, Ember. 30 May. 2021.

3 SCARRED LIKE THE MOUNTAINSIDE

Sometimes, I think that the only reason I ever accepted my scars as something beautiful rather than something that should be covered, is because like me, the mountainside where I grew up is covered in scars, and I think that they are beautiful.

Like mine, some are man-made, and others are natural and couldn't be helped. Where I have scars from the bad days, the mountain that faces mine is covered in burns after a driver carelessly through a cigarette out of a car window on a dry summer. We never heard of anyone being held accountable for the damage they caused, despite the fact that their mindless act filled the sky with a layer of thick, black smoke and killed the wildflowers and gorse bushes. Although that was fifteen years ago and the scars have mostly faded, you can still see the shadows of them in the gorse bushes that grew in place of the ones that died. Stonechats and wild hares can be seen playing in them now.

My mountain, home to Gwynus Camping & Caravan Park, has a huge hole in the side of it after Owain, the owner of the caravan park, dug it out to make a road that now goes around the campsite. He put a fence in front of it recently, I assume kids were trying to climb it and he wanted to stop them. I was never the kid to do anything like that, I don't even think I ever climbed a tree, never mind rock climb up the side a hole in a mountain. I was always too afraid of banging my head.

Where I have my hydrocephalus scars and a shunt that drains fluid like a constant river running through me, as you walk up the lane you can see where the edges of the road have been worn away into tiny cliff faces from sheep's hooves as they climb up and down to avoid approaching cars. Whenever it rains these cliff faces become waterfalls sending streams down the mountain, draining the water into the cattle-grid at the bottom.

3Birchall, Ember. 24 Jul. 2022.

4 THE KESTREL

It has only been since we returned from lockdown that I took up bird watching. I'd only started taking photography seriously the autumn before, and when restrictions were still in place so all we could do was spend hours watching the bird table, it became the perfect opportunity for me to learn all the settings on my new camera.

Through bird watching, I was able to learn how to set up my camera to capture the perfect photo of robin while it flapped its wings as it landed on the bird table. From then on, I started noting down the different birds I'd see through my caravan window. When the restrictions lifted and we were able to travel around to new places, the newfound hobby came with us. I've seen all sorts out on my adventures with my camera, chaffinches, stonechats, a grey wagtail over on Parc Glynnifon. My favourite photo of all so far, is the kestrel that I saw just as I was approaching the cattle grid halfway up the mountain.

With its big, beautiful wings spread out wide, moving so fast that I wasn't even sure that I'd managed to get a photo, and even if I had I didn't think it would be in focus. Something delicious had caught its eye, a mouse maybe, or a smaller bird hiding in the safety of the heather and gorse bushes. I hope it was a mouse, I've never liked them, not since the year the campsite was overrun with them after the sheep field flooded, forcing them all to evacuate and move in to tents and caravans. I swear one of them ran over me while I was asleep, but dad said it was probably just the fur on my teddy bear or one of the dogs. When we found one in the trap under my bed the next morning, I ran off and showered, refusing to come back into the caravan until the corpse was gone. If the kestrel was eyeing up its next meal, for that night, I hope that it was a mouse and not some cute little stonechat or wagtail.

It was only when I got back to my caravan and plugged my camera into my laptop that I was able to clearly see the photos, the browns, and blacks in the kestrel's feathers as its wings spread out as wide as they could reach. I took loads of photos, in college my photography teacher had drilled into us to at least take three photos of everything so that if the first one is bad at least one of them will turn out good, but I must have taken over twenty photos of the kestrel as it circled – looking for a mouse in the long grass.

4Birchall, Ember. 23 Apr. 2020.

5 CROSSING THE CATTLE GRID

It's halfway up the mountain that I decide to step carefully as I cross over the big metal cattle grid that divides the land between the two farmers who have decided to call this mountain home.

For me, this cattle grid is anxiety and excitement all rolled up into one big rush of adrenaline. When I was three or four years old, this cattle grid is where I got my foot stuck while out on a walk with my dad and our Chihuahuas. I can still hear him telling me to wait as he tied the dogs lead to the gate before coming back to get me, but I thought I could do it. Now, at the ripe old age of twenty-three, I'm still careful about where I place my feet when I'm trying to cross, even though I know that it's now physically impossible for me to get my size fives between the bars. There's still always the anxiety of 'what if'.

This cattle grid is also where when I was sixteen, I followed Michael up what used to be the golf course but will now forever be the place where I learned I have a fear of cattle after they followed us while we were out on a walk. Even though that was six years ago, and the cattle are gone, I'm still careful when I go out with my camera just in case there's a cow somewhere that I haven't seen despite there being nowhere for one to hide.

This is where now, I take a second to enjoy the view, to take some photos which I repeat to myself like I did last year that I should get these printed as postcards but then never do. Photos of the cerulean sea in the distance which disappears between two mountains, the crumbling stone cottage down by the main road, the new luxury houses off in the distance, and the luscious green and earthy brown mountains like the one that looks like a sleeping giant under all the dirt and stone.

5Birchall, Ember. 24 Jul. 2022.

6 ST BEUNO'S CHURCH

When I climb the mountain and keep in line with the cattle grid, in the distance I can see the turning for St Beuno's Church. Dad had been telling me about it for years, but it was only the autumn before lockdown that we decided to venture over there to go and walk amongst the broken head stones.

There's something oddly calming about walking through cemeteries surrounded by silence as no one around you dares to speak. The only sound inside the gate, is that of footsteps on the stone path leading to the church door. Even the birds go mute as they pass over the hallowed grounds.

Apart from an actor that dad vaguely remembers from the sixties, we don't know anyone who is buried there, but I find it interesting to see the progression of burials as over time funerals have changed from simply covering the corpse in stones to eventually burying them beneath the earth. I got some good photos that first time we went, of the mounds of stone and dirt. Before going inside, dad led me up the slope to see Rupert Davies, the actor he mentioned. Apparently, he played a detective on Maigret, but I've never seen it. I wouldn't even know where to find it online anymore.

After paying our respects to a well-loved stranger, we went inside the church where the floors were carpeted in layers of straw and the donations tin waits eagerly by the door for a handful of loose change. Unlike cemeteries, I never felt like I could settle in a church, so I didn't stay inside long before returning to the comfort of the quiet graveyard. I stayed long enough to see that the notice board was still in use, highlighting that services are still being held monthly in the church, on Christmas Eve and to celebrate Lammas in August. On one of the walls is an ancient wall painting depicting two people, but I'm not sure who they are.

When dad finished whatever, it was that he was doing in the church we went for a walk through the sheep field so I could try and get some sunset photos. They came out pretty good, I still have them saved somewhere. I remember I was surprised by how calm the sheep were as we walked through their field.

6BIRCHALL, EMBER. 29 OCT. 2019.

7 THE MAN OF THE MOUNTAIN

The Man of the Mountain has been here since the earth decided to make mountains in North Wales - in the land of the giants. From the lane leading up to the caravan park, you can see where one of the giants lay down to fall asleep and then became covered in dirt and rock.

There is a farm on his neck now, at night when I'm walking the dogs, I can see the farmhouse lights in the distance. Growing up, I used to wonder what would happen to the farmhouse, the farmers, and their livestock when the giant eventually decided that it was time to wake up from his long slumber. There is another farm over on his feet as well. As a kid, I could see their lights by standing on the top of the slide on the back field. Some nights it would look like the farmhouses were talking to each other in morse code by blinking their living room lights. I always wanted to try and work out what they were saying but by the time it was dark enough, I'd be called in because it was getting late.

I remember that used to be one of my favourite games as a kid, with my dad and step mum when we'd be out in the car somewhere, we'd spend hours looking around at the mountains and imagining what could be buried underneath them to make them into the shape that they are. At the back of the caravan park, by the field where the sheep are kept, there is another mountain that dad says looks like an alien spaceship had landed and disguised to blend in with the mountains. Growing up, he would often tell me that the aliens have come and were looking for him, but they had parked their spaceship and forgotten where they'd left it. My step mum would laugh at our overactive imaginations before joining in, saying that the mountain next to it looks like Pride Rock from The Lion King.

7Birchall, Ember. 24 Jul. 2022.

8 NANT GWRTHEYRN

On the drive over to Nant Gwrtheyrn, we pass the mountain that dad says looks like an alien spaceship. Growing up, he would often tell me that the aliens have come and were looking for him, but they had parked their spaceship and forgotten where they'd left it.

We pass this mountain every time we go to the heritage centre by the village of Llithfaen. I don't remember the first time we went to Nant Gwrtheyrn. I just remember that she was there and that she was happy. She loved the long and winding roads that felt like a roller coaster lost in nature, leading us further and further down the mountain until we thought we were going to fall off the edge. You never realise how far up you are. I remember looking through the back window, I couldn't even see over the edge. All I could see was the luscious blue and the pearly white waves coming towards us.

Continuing the drive down to the Nant, the view of a clear blue sea is replaced with the greens and browns of the spruce tree forest on either side of the road. The first time we went, we thought we were lost as we kept going further and further down, getting lost in the forest. When we looked through the side windows, we couldn't even see an end to the trees, we didn't know how it was possible. How could so many trees fit on the side of a cliff?

At the bottom we arrived at the car park, in front of which is a row of cottages that we later learned are mostly available to rent for holidays and weddings. That is except for the first one on the far end that has been decorated like how it would have been in the 1930s and shows what life was like for the miners who worked there. □I couldn't wrap my head around how small it was the first time we went. Dad was amazed by the tin bath that had been placed in front of the fireplace, I was fascinated by the tapestry made by a nine-year-old girl with her name, age, numbers one to ten, and the alphabet on it. I wouldn't have the patience to learn how to do that.

It's changed a lot since the first time we went, most of the forest has been cut down now, there's a cafe there too, it's expensive, but it's nice enough. I remember she liked it there, when she came in her wheelchair the staff were amazing at trying to help us find somewhere to sit where there would be plenty of space and making sure that we weren't too far away from the disabled toilets just in case.

Whenever we went to the Nant, she'd look down at the bottom at the stoney beach. She always wanted to go down there, but it was too steep for her. After she died, my dad and I took a walk down and picked up a rock to take back to the caravan with us. It's still at the back of the caravan near her TV with NANT GWRTHEYRN and the date we walked down written on it in sharpie.

We've been down there a few times now, down the narrow and steep slope to the beach. The dogs love it, especially when after the steep walk, they get to cool off in the sea. Apparently, there are sea lions there, but I've never seen any.

I walked down alone the last time we went, I wanted to get some photos of the beach while there was nobody else down there. Dad waited at the cafe at the top. It doesn't take me too long to walk down, get some photos of the isolated landscape, and then climb back up again.

8Birchall, Ember. 20 Apr. 2021.

9 RED DRAGONS & EASTER EGG HUNTS

Once I reach the top of the lane, I stop for another minute and admire the view. This is one of the most changed areas of the caravan park over the years.

There has always been a flag here, with its red dragon flying proudly in the air, I remember it always being a popular hiding place when the mums on the caravan park held Easter Egg hunts across the site. The clue would read something about where the dragon flies and we would all go running to the entrance where the flagpole is.

The old static that used to be Owain's office is gone now. It used to be where people could check in or rent golf clubs, but there is a large wooden cabin there now that he used to live in with his wife when they were renovating the farmhouse. He rents it out now for weekends to people who want to enjoy the view but keep the luxury of a comfortable bed instead of a caravan sofa and a sleeping bag.

The original park has also gone now, it was a death trap so that's probably a good thing, and there's the park on the back field now which has three swings instead of two, but that old park is one of the first things that I remember about this campsite. Racing my friends to the swings, first place getting the safe swing on the end away from the slide, second place either having to go on the wonky swing and risk banging their knee on the side of the slide or waiting on the floor until it was their turn. Making newcomers aware of the swing situation and making them wait on the top of the slide until the safe one was free. It was fun, but we could never swing too high because of the old static behind us, we were always scared of coming off and falling through the rusty old roof.

Standing here, I can still imagine her walking towards me with one of the Chihuahua's to let me know that it's time to come in now because tea is nearly done. Everyone would run to her wanting to say hello to whichever dog she had brought with her, which would usually lead to the dog hiding behind her legs or begging to be picked up because they were anxious around crowds of screaming kids. Now as an adult, I have never related to anything more in my life, maybe my spirit animal is a Chihuahua? It would make a lot of sense, I'm 5'2" with a 7' attitude, yet shy around crowds of people even when I know them.

They were the good times, as we grew with the caravan park and my friends eventually left and moved on, those are the days that make me want to keep going there, to see the ghosts of everyone who left.

9Birchall, Ember. 20 Jul. 2022.

10 THE SUMMER OF BMX'S

I pass the park and cut through the front field towards the stone field, by now I can hear country music, which is probably my dad testing the CD player to make sure that it hasn't been damaged by the winter weather - the amount of rain over the past few months could explain why Dolly Parton has suddenly developed a stutter when she's singing the chorus of Jolene.

The stone field is smaller than the others, but it's where the shower block is, along with a big roundabout full of plants and trees in the centre - another of our favourite hiding places when we were growing up.

My caravan is over in the back left corner next to the door into the women's showers. Dad thought it would be handy when I was little or when we brought my friends with us, but as she started to decline, having the disabled shower just a few short feet away became a blessing. Especially when she was too weak to walk and needed to be carried, or at least held up as she made her way around.

This field is not all bad memories though. This field is one of the places where I learned to ride my bike. Since this field is all stone and no grass, and surprisingly flat considering we are on top of a mountain, it was the perfect place to learn to ride a bike without stabilisers. There were huge stones back then though, not the small gravel that it's today. She would keep the first-aid box full of Sudecreme and plasters for all my scrapes and bruises when I would inevitably fall off my bike.

I can still picture the summer when I was eleven or twelve and I brought my old BMX up here because mum had bought me a new one for my birthday. The chain needed a link taking out of it and every now and then it would fall off without warning, often causing a crash into a swing post or a fence, I'm lucky I never crashed into anyone's caravan. By then we were at the age where the boys wanted to prove themselves as tough and strong, so would repeatedly try to fix the chain so I could continue riding. By the end of the day when it was time to go inside, they were all covered in oil.

11 WE WERE ONE OF THE FIRST

We were one of the first. My dad, my step mum and me. Before we arrived, there was nothing here but a crumbling farmhouse, ten static caravans that have been here forever and Owain, the old cowboy by the front gate who was just as shocked as my dad when we first arrived. It's strange to think how much has changed in the past twenty years.

The farmhouse has been redecorated, there are now fifty caravans spread out around the edges of four fields, the original swing set has been torn down and a new one rebuilt in its place, but my tourer caravan has remained in the same spot in the corner of the second field for so long that I now consider it a static. Oh, and the old cowboy still walks around the site every day - I don't think I've ever seen him stood still.

Over the hedge behind my caravan, I can see one of the new luxury lodges. It doesn't feel the same. For me the point of coming here was to leave luxuries behind, to say goodbye to signal and reconnect with the open skies, to try and fly with the kestrel or outrun the wild hare, to shower with spiders on the ceiling and to have the electrics cut out when you forget that you can't use the heater and the kettle at the same time. What is luxurious about that?

Surrounded by second-hand tourers and ancient statics that have been here since the dawn of time, awnings that have been damaged by fierce winds, these lodges don't look right.

10Birchall, Ember. 20 Jul. 2022.

12 HER GARDEN

The garden outside the caravan is dead now. Well, mostly. At one time it was full of life, full of greenery and growth, with a bird house and table, we would be entertained all day looking at all the brightly coloured birds that would come looking for a feast - robins, sparrows, bluetits, and magpies all crowding around for a mouthful of seeds.

Now, the wood has rotted, and the bird table is on the floor, the bird house is missing its roof, and someone has stolen some of the flowers out of their beds. She would cry is she could see it now, maybe that's why it rains so much when we're here. She's trying to water the flowers that have been dead for as long as she has, she's trying to bring the garden back to life with no success. Last year we tried to help her, we bought her new flowers and dug up the weeds, but then she became so happy, and the sun shone so brightly that it burnt the petals on the roses we bought her. Maybe this year we can try again.

The barbeque is also gone now, I can't remember the last time we used it, but the stand had rusted so much that it could no longer stand on its own. Like her, it would fall on even the slightest attempt. I used to love the summer holidays when it was just us three, the smell of burgers and hotdogs would lure me in from the park, dad would show off his cooking skills as she would shake her head and pour me a drink. We would have the CDs playing country music in the background and the sun burning our shoulders, it was perfect.

I always remember her sitting on her swing reading a book, usually a Catherine Cookson, while dad was always standing near the barbeque waiting for us to ask for more, and I would either be sat at the table getting covered in ketchup or on the floor with the dogs. I found a Catherine Cookson book the other day; someone had left it in the launderette along with a handful of others.

If we still had the swing, I could sit there like she did and get lost between the pages.

11BIRCHALL, EMBER. 23 AUG. 2011.

13 PWLLHELI MARKET

The day we bought her roses, dad decided to start our trip into town by going for a walk along the high street and then visit the market on the way back to the car, so instead of stopping to have a look around, we brushed past what remains of the market after most of the stall holders shut up shop after the pandemic and walked up Stryd Moch towards the High Street.

On the way, we passed the pub that she loved, with its strawberry milkshakes and beer-battered onion rings that were so big you could wear them as a bracelet. We used to love going in there for some dinner after doing some shopping. I remember one time; it was just me and her in town having a girl's day while dad cleaned the caravan and looked after the dogs. We stopped in there for a milkshake before eventually going back to my dad. I've still got the Snow-White bedding we bought that day — it's always handy to keep a spare set.

We turned right into the High Street and passed the bank towards what I call 'charity shop central'. There are only three or four, but it always feels like more when dad feels the need to go into every single one. After having a sort out at the caravan and deciding to get rid of a few things to clear up some space, I carried a carrier bag of shirts and shorts with me to donate, but it was like he was trying to find the perfect place to part with them. In the end he settled on Tenovus which made sense considering it's a cancer charity. It was hard to part with them, but the woman behind the counter was happy about the donation which made things a bit easier.

We bought the flowers for her garden from the market on the way back to the car. We just managed to make it to the stall before the woman started to pack everything away into her van. She hadn't brought loads; it was near the end of summer, so she didn't see the sense in bringing too many. Especially when they'd all be dead soon. Luckily for us, the ones that were left were the kind that come up every year, so we wouldn't have to keep going out to buy more, just move them to a different pot every now and then.

12Birchall, Ember. 27 Jul. 2011.

14 THE BEGINNING OF THE TOURISM TRADE

According to Owain's biography, Tryweryn: A Nation Awakes, it was his mum who decided to join the tourism trade, first she just rented out a spare bedroom and eventually she was able to get a static. From there the caravan park grew. When he first got married and had kids, he was living in one of them for a while. There is quite a few statics now compared to back then.

When I was in college studying Media, I was enjoying photography, so my mum bought me a camera. I brought it with me one time and when I went back home, I took my photos to college to show my teacher. He said they remind him of a caravan park that he goes to called Gwynus. It turns out that he has a static here. I have never seen him though. Growing up that was the one field we would never go in, none of my friends had statics so we never had a reason to.

When my dad used to work for Owain, doing odd jobs in exchange for site fees, I went in one of the statics with my step mum to help her clean it ready for a family who were renting it for the weekend. He still rents that one out I think, but his wife does all the cleaning in there now. I remember it feeling bigger on the inside with all its bedrooms and private bathroom, I dusted and polished everywhere while she made the beds. We had it done in no time, it felt like. Then dad met us with the car to carry all the old bedding round to the launderette.

A few years later I ended up staying the night in that static caravan. My mum and stepdad had decided that they needed a weekend away and decided to rent it out for the weekend. I stayed a night in there with them, but I prefer my own bed and returned to my own caravan the next night, meeting up with them for breakfast in the morning. My mum's friend and her two sons had come with my mum and stepdad that weekend and I didn't like the sons much, they kept stealing my stuff and I walked out after the first night to go and stay with my dad and step mum. We took them to see Nant Gwrtheyrn that weekend. I loved showing my mum some of the hidden gems that I've been visiting all these years, she said I'm like a different person at the caravan. Her friend and her sons didn't enjoy it at all - they weren't interested in history and were annoyed when we lost signal on our phones.

15 THE FAMILY FUN DAY

There are quite a few sheep in the field at the back today, and some black lambs who are new. They're all so tiny, they can't be that old. Owain must have left the gate open this morning because when we woke up there was a big white one standing outside the front of our caravan.

From the gate leading into the field, you can see the mountain that looks like an alien spaceship that I mentioned earlier, and if you walk through the gate and keep going down to the far end, you can see the faint remains of a Bronze Age Fort lifting the dirt into circles.

I still remember that scorching summer afternoon when we used that field to hold a family fun-day for all the campers that were there for the summer holidays. 2009 I think it was. We had fancy dress competitions, food and book stalls, loads of different races and games, my favourite bit was throwing the wet sponges at all the dads. Mine didn't volunteer to sit in a garden chair for the game so when it was over, I chased him with a bucket of water and a sponge. I don't think there was ever another day like that, it became too much hassle trying to set it up.☐I still have an album full of photos somewhere, I think they might be in the drawer under the TV at the front of the caravan.

There's an old static in there too - they seem to be everywhere. I remember one night when we were playing man hunt, a few of us climbed over the gate and went exploring. It wasn't plugged into any sort of electric so it was dark in there and we could barely see. We tried using the torches on our phones, but they didn't make much of a difference. I just remember it being dark and moldy with random scraps of wood everywhere.

Owain's son ended up renovating it not long after we went inside, that must have been what all the pieces of wood were for. He and his wife were living in there with their new-born while they saved up to buy a house

13Birchall, Ember. 26 Aug. 2020.

16 THE NEW FIELD

Turning left I enter the back field; this is where most of our summers took place once the new swing set was built and ready to be used. I was there the day my dad replaced the rope on the swings with metal chains. There's a giant metal gate guarding the entrance, that's for when Owain is transferring the sheep from the field to the farm and back again, it keeps them out of people's awnings.

Through the gate, there are caravans around the edge of the field, with a toilets block and launderette to the left of the entrance. We weren't supposed to hide there either, but when it was getting colder in the evenings, the launderette was warm - especially if the dryer had been on. There are books in there now, as I said earlier, I picked a few up the other day while waiting for the washer, I swapped them for DVDs and board games after having a clear out in the caravan. Somebody has already taken some of the DVDs.

I keep walking past the launderette, to the second corner of this square field. Between two Hobby caravans is the entrance to the newer field right at the back. It's only small, I think it only holds fifteen caravans and they're all pretty close together. I used to have a few friends on that field, but eventually they preferred a Wi-Fi connection over running around trying not to fall and scrape our knees after 7pm because we knew if we went back to our caravans for a plaster then our parents would tell us to stay inside now because it's getting late.

Dad has a photo somewhere of the field before the path and the caravan spaces were added - back when it was just long green grass and hay bales making it look like something from a postcard, or a painting in an art gallery somewhere. If I was talented in the ways of paint and canvas, I'd love to take an easel and paint some of the landscapes, I guess that's why I love photography so much, because within a few seconds I can capture a photo of a perfect landscape instead of sitting outside in the cold for hours.

14Birchall, Ember. 24 Aug. 2011.

17 BEFORE HEALTH & SAFETY

Back before health and safety, a time when wet paper towels could cure broken bones - the swing set on the back field was the heart of the chaos that took place over the summer months.

During the day it would be transformed into an obstacle course, as we played 'the floor is lava' and would make our way across the swings, and up onto the top of the slide. If you touched the floor you'd have to start over. Or sometimes we would use the swings to try to launch ourselves into space, to see who could swing the highest or jump the furthest. But as the sun began to dim, leaving us alone with just the one light in the field over by the launderette, our games of man hunt would begin. We would split ourselves into two teams, the swing set would be our base. Being there the longest, everyone wanted me on their teams because I knew all of the best hiding places, and I almost always made it back to the base without being seen.

I remember this one time, back when I was going through my emo phase and was constantly wearing black, I lay down in the long grass in the dark, I was practically invisible, and I waited for my friends to come running by before sitting up and shouting, scaring the lot of them. Except, I didn't realise that one of my friends had her six-year-old sister, she ran all the way back to their caravan crying. I remember buying her a cheap toy from town the next day to try and make it up to her.

It makes me sad when I walk past it now, most of my friends here have left and moved on. Like Wendy, John, and Michael, they left this Neverland to go home and grow up.

The last I heard from anyone, most have not been camping or caravanning since, while others left for caravan parks with a better Wi-Fi connection or where there is more on the site than the excitement of feeding the new-born lambs in the Spring.

15BIRCHALL, EMBER. 26 AUG. 2020.

18 CRICCIETH

As I continue walking past the swing set, instead of turning right and leaving the field through the gate that I entered, I walk straight ahead and leave through a second gate that brings you out by the farm and the lane leading towards Owain's house. Walking through the gate, the sound of my footsteps on the gravel is accompanied by the all-too-familiar singing of the caravan park's resident robin. I turn around to see him, tilting his head admiring the stranger who stands around taking photos of him, perched on the fence post that supports the gate I'd just walked through.

He hops around, following me as I pass the side of the static field and the farm. He's cute as he whistles and tilts his head from side to side, his little red breast contrasting the pale grey of the gravel floor and the faded wooden fence that surrounds the perimeter of the statics field. He reminds me of the little robin that I saw in Criccieth when I went for a drive out with dad. It was one of the first times I've been there, but after being stuck inside with lockdown for so long we wanted to go to as many different places as possible with my camera before we were sent into another lockdown.

We were sitting on the balcony of a café by the beach when a little robin perched itself on the wall by our table. He stayed there for a while, I pulled some bread off my sandwich and set it on the table for him, and he pecked at it before spreading his little wings and fluttering off to patrol the other tables that were full of people, mainly children dropping food on the floor. He was a cute little thing, the way his head tilted as dad tried to whistle to him. I wonder if he could understand whatever it was that dad was trying to say. I wonder if dad was actually saying anything.

I try whistling to this robin that is following me past the side of the statics field and the old farmhouse, I must be doing something right because he tilts his head to listen to me before fluttering off when he hears the noise of a lamb in the small pen.

16Birchall, Ember. 24 Aug. 2020.

19 THE TIME WE FED THE LAMBS

As the robin flies away, I pass the farm on my left which, although we were not supposed to, became one of the more popular hiding places for our late-night games of man hunt.

There's a sheep pen next to it, only small, this is where Owain keeps the lambs who need bottle feeding, usually because their mother died during the birth, or occasionally it's because they've been born with some sort of defect like Bentley, a lamb who was here a few years ago who was born with a crooked neck.

Whenever I walk past here, I always stop to see if there are any lambs this year. There are a few black ones here this time, I noticed some in the main field when I was walking past earlier, but these ones came running towards the gate that is holding them in place as I walked by. There is also a white one in with the mix, I wonder why these ones have been kept separated.

Their wagging tails behind them reminds me of a joke my dad always says when he walks past them, about the nursery rhyme Little Bow Peep. All this time I thought he had come up with it himself, but then I recently discovered that it's actually the 'It's in The Book' sketch by Johnny Standley. He does that a lot, my dad, now that I have access to the internet when I have a song stuck in my head, I've realised that many of the songs I grew up singing with the belief that my dad had come up with them, were actually big hits in the 1940s and 50s. Like how I was nineteen when my mind was blown when I heard You Are My Sunshine on an advert, or that Bang Bang (My Baby Shot Me Down) was an actual song, sung by Nancy Sinatra in 1966.

The last time my dad came with me to visit the lambs, it was a few years ago and there were three in the pen. Owain had said we could have a go at feeding them with a bottle. We both ended up covered in poo and dirt, dad in his off-white pants got it the worst, especially when it took him three or four goes in the launderette to get out the red dye that was on the lambs. That was his karma for letting me believe that one of my favourite songs was made up by him, not by Kevin Johnson.

17BIRCHALL, EMBER. 28 OCT. 2019.

20 THE OLD FARMHOUSE

I carry on past the lambs. Now, the farmhouse is on my right and there's a chicken coop on my left. I don't know why he bothers fencing them in, they always manage to find a way out and end up roaming the caravan park all day. They're often in our garden looking for bird seeds.

In front of the chicken coop are three cars that I'm guessing, belong to Owain. There's at least one new one compared to last year, I feel like he has a new car every time I see him.

I normally see him around here, collecting eggs that he sells in packs of six, or just leaving the house. I remember my dad taking me in there once before the renovations had begun, I can't remember why, but now when I knock on asking for pound coins for the launderette, the kitchen and dining room that I can see from the door looks amazing. All new and modern, unlike it's rough and stony exterior. I don't think a modern exterior would look right, thank God it's a listed building. I don't think modern would suit the aesthetic of the caravan park with its stone walls covered in moss and wooden fences held together with chicken wire.

I carry on walking past the crumbling pig pen next to the house. If I continue straight across then I'll soon arrive at the cattle grid where when we cross it in the car, the dogs back because they know where we are. Instead, I go up the slope at the back of the pig pen, up to the front field where I used to know everyone but now, I barely know anyone.

I've tried to find a few of them on Facebook over the years, after the BBM trend died down, but we never exchanged surnames, this wasn't the place for those, and do you know how many Aarons there are? There were at least two here, so I wouldn't stand a chance in finding any of them. I wonder if they've tried to look for me. I doubt it, but sometimes I wonder. They've probably forgotten me now; it's been so long since we were all together.

Some kids run past me as I make my way back up the middle of the field towards my caravan, one of them with a bike like my old BMX and I can see the cycle starting over again. They're going to have the time of their lives up here. I just know it.

21 THE WOODPECKER RETURNS

I return from my walk and get comfortable on the sofa, I'm just about to take the SIM card out of my camera when the susurrus of long since forgotten wings breaks through the silence of the lost signal on the TV. Cautiously at first, hidden away in the leaves of the large oak tree at the back of the caravan, watching over us, and staying silent in case we come outside.

She knocks against the oak tree. Once. Twice. Disturbing the silence and looking curiously for a response. We both know better than to go outside and disturb her. Instead, I attach my zoom lens to my camera and aim it through the partially open window on the side of the caravan.

After another pause, she leaves the cover of the oak and buries her claws into the branches of the long since dead birch tree next to it where I'm able to take a photo.

From here she can be seen. From here, my dad and I can see her pied black and white plumage and red patch on her lower abdomen. A welcome sight. She knocks again against the branch. This time to call her young. Two. Three. Four more join her. Their eyes staring eagerly at the crumbling bird table below them. Earlier today I had filled it with all their favourite nuts and seeds. A feast.

I reach for my camera once more. The woodpecker has returned.

18Birchall, Ember. 17 Jun. 2021.

RAISED BY MOUNTAINS

WHEN I WANT TO WRITE A LOVE POEM

COMING FEBRUARY 2024…

RAISED BY MOUNTAINS

WHEN I WANT TO WRITE A LOVE POEM

"YOU'VE GOT A FAST CAR
IS IT FAST ENOUGH SO WE CAN FLY AWAY?"
- FAST CAR, TRACY CHAPMAN

I listen to the song that reminds
me of you and think about how within
seconds my eyes are closed and my
hips are swaying from side to side
to the sad guitar of the opening verse.
I sing silently into the night. I drink
vodka. I dance around my room in the
dark with the ghost of you — and when
the beat hits, when the drums awaken
the adrenaline in me at 1am when I can't
sleep, I'm reminded of the adrenaline I
had during that teenage first kiss — or a
few years later, on the night we went for a
drive — or the night we wrote our own
genres by the invasive streetlamp light —
or the birthday you offered to pick me up
to go for a drive at 11 o'clock at night. You're
the song that I can't get out of my head,
you are my sad guitar, my soft beating drum
that comes alive for the chorus, my grand piano.

ABOUT THE AUTHOR

Ember Birchall is a writer and poet who uses their surroundings and experiences as an influence for their work. They have a Bachelor of Arts in English Literature and Creative Writing from Staffordshire University and a passion for exploring their hometown as well as favourite travel locations through poetry, prose, and photography. They live in Warrington, UK with their family and four dogs, Teddy, Tula, Oliver, and Paddy. You can find more of their work on Amazon or by following them on TikTok @loverofwordsandrhyme.

Printed in Great Britain
by Amazon